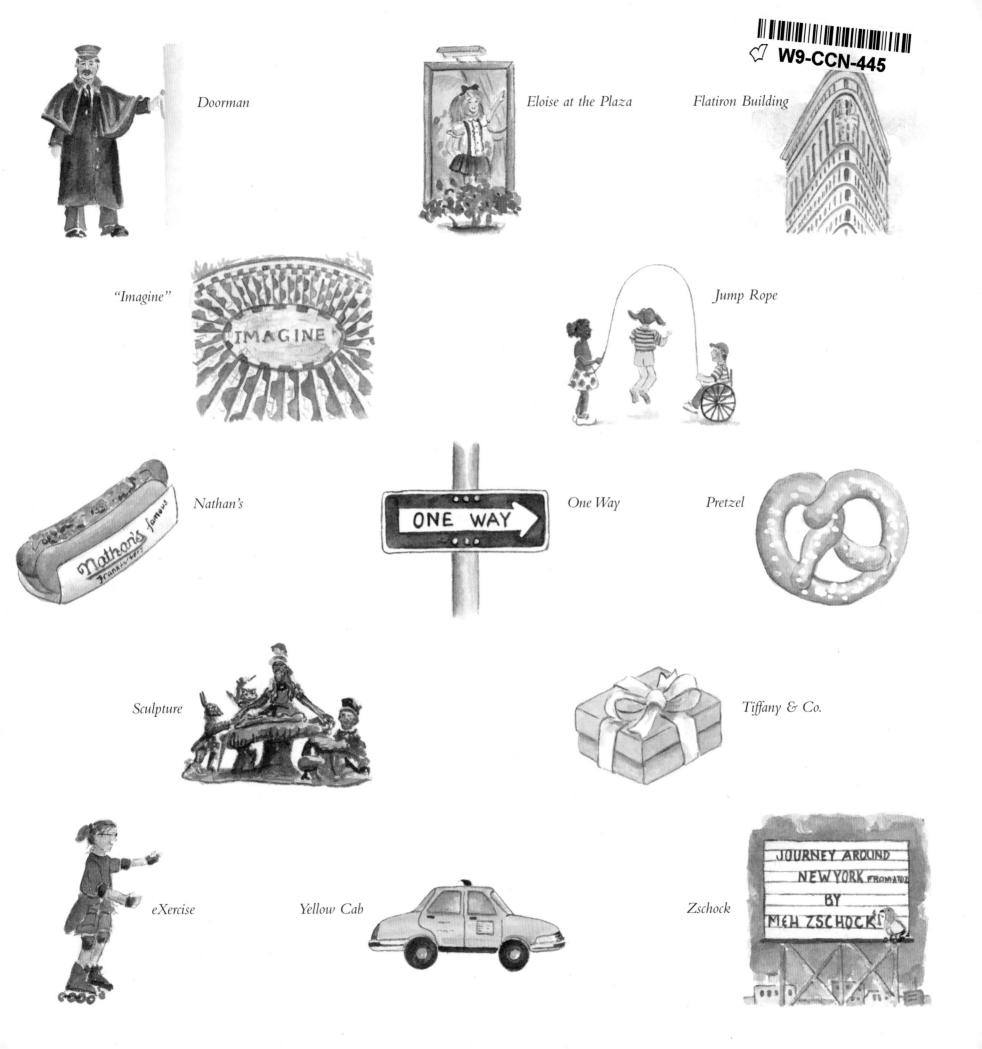

Doorman

Eloise at the Plaza

Flatiron Building

"Imagine"

Jump Rope

Nathan's

One Way

Pretzel

Sculpture

Tiffany & Co.

eXercise

Yellow Cab

Zschock

JOURNEY AROUND NEW YORK FROM A TO Z
BY M&H ZSCHOCK

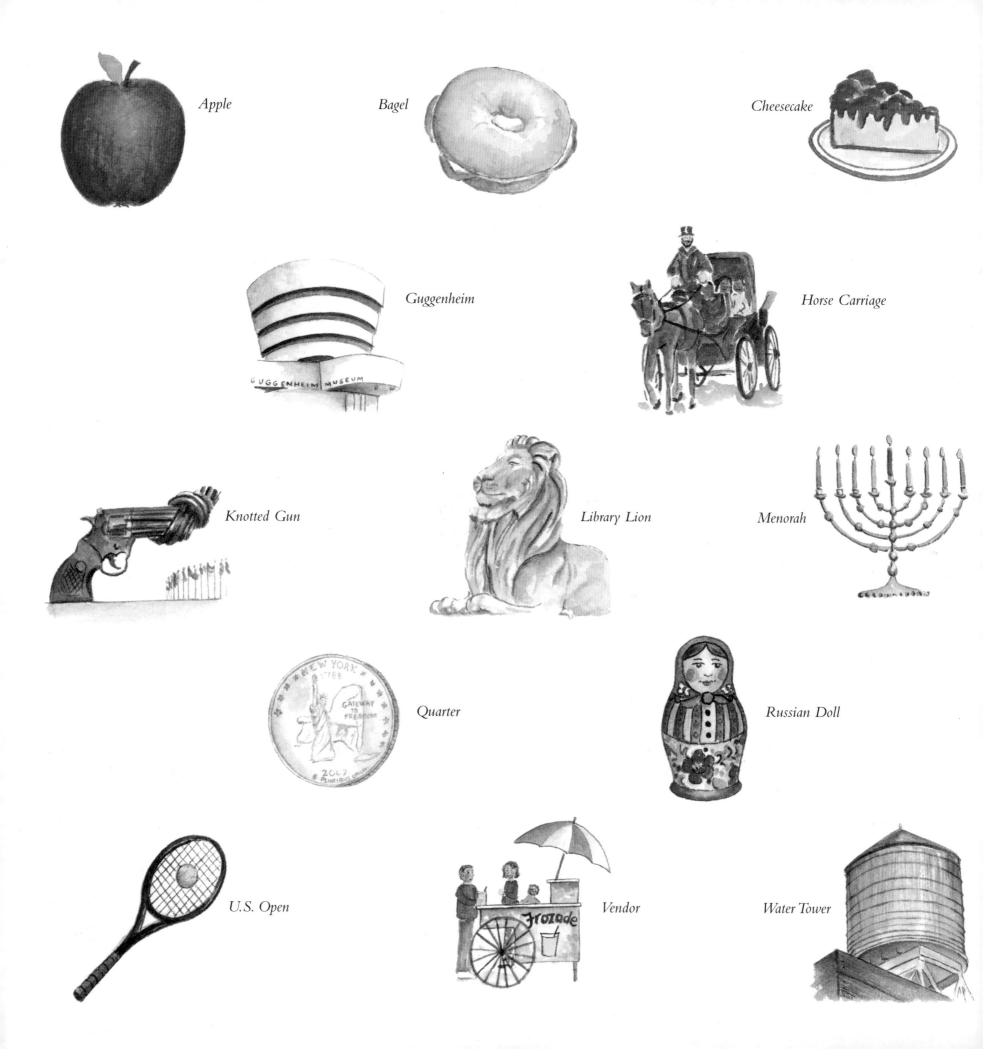

Apple

Bagel

Cheesecake

Guggenheim

Horse Carriage

Knotted Gun

Library Lion

Menorah

Quarter

Russian Doll

U.S. Open

Vendor

Water Tower

Journey Around

New York

from A to Z

by Martha & Heather Zschock

COMMONWEALTH EDITIONS

Beverly, Massachusetts

To our wonderful family

and to twins, teamwork, and hope

With special thanks to our Journey friends, Webster and Katie Bull, Shawna Mullen, John Hartley, Memories in Color, Christel and Natalie Burkard, Arlynn Willis, Scott Kerry, Pam Nobili, Stephen Turtell of the Museum of the City of New York, John Beatty of The Cotton Club, and Lauren Daniluk of the New Victory Theater.

Commonwealth Editions
An imprint of Memoirs Unlimited, Inc.
21 Lothrop Street
Beverly, MA 01915
Visit us at www.commonwealtheditions.com

ISBN 1-889833-32-0

10 9 8 7 6 5 4 3 2 1

Printed in Korea

GREETINGS, MY FRIENDS, AND
Welcome to New York!

THE BIG APPLE, uptown and down, is a vast melting pot of cultures, hopes, and dreams. The city has an amazingly rich and interesting past, and a present full of exciting opportunities for all.

Looking at New York City today, it is difficult to imagine the area as it once was—covered in a lush forest full of animal life. When Giovanni Verrazano first sailed into New York Harbor in 1524, the island of Manhattan was called *Manna-hata* by the Native Americans who used it as a hunting and fishing ground. When the Dutch West India Company settled in the area in 1625, it became known as New Amsterdam. Later, under British rule, it was called New York, and the name stuck.

As millions of hopeful immigrants arrived, and technology advanced, the city continued to grow upward and outward. Today it is a cultural, financial, and educational center which millions of New Yorkers call home.

Come, let's explore the Big Apple, the "city that never sleeps," and take a journey around New York City!

1. Times Square
2. Wall Street
3. Coney Island
4. Chinatown
5. Empire State Building
6. Fifth Avenue &
   Saks Fifth Avenue
7. New York
   Botanical Garden
8. USS *Intrepid*
9. Statue of Liberty
10. Radio City Music Hall
11. South Street Seaport
12. American Museum of
    Natural History
13. Lincoln Center
14. Central Park
15. Bronx Zoo
16. Lower East Side
17. Brooklyn Bridge
18. Staten Island Ferry
19. Macy's
20. Rockefeller Center
    & Channel Gardens
21. Flushing Meadows
    Corona Park &
    Unisphere
22. Former site of the
    Twin Towers
23. United Nations
24. Harlem
25. Metropolitan Museum
    of Art
26. Cathedral of St. John
    the Divine
27. Yankee Stadium
28. Grand Central
    Terminal

Westchester

NEW JERSEY

Long Island Sound

BRONX

Hudson River

MANHATTAN

East River

QUEENS

Upper New York Bay

BROOKLYN

Jamaica Bay

STATEN ISLAND

Lower New York Bay

N

W — E

S

NEW YORK CITY

Audiences applaud actors and actresses.

GEORGE
·M·
COHAN
1878-1942

Give my regards to Broadway

AS THE CURTAIN RISES ON BROADWAY, excitement grows for eager audiences. With plays like *Peter and Wendy* and lavish musicals like *The Lion King*, Broadway is the heart of American theater and home to actors and actresses seeking "the big time." Although movies drew crowds away for a time, Broadway shows are now more popular than ever. The New Victory Theater is New York's first theater with performances especially for kids.

New Victory Theater, Times Square
Inset: George M. Cohan Statue, Times Square
Detail: The Great White Way

Broadway is nicknamed "The Great White Way" for the many lights sparkling on its theater marquees.

Brokers buy and sell billions.

WALL STREET, named for a wall built by the Dutch to protect early settlers against attacks, is now the city's financial center. At the New York and American stock exchanges, stock brokers buy and sell shares of the world's largest companies. Those who expect good times are called "bulls," while "bears" predict trouble ahead. Arturo Di Modica's sculpture *Charging Bull* is a symbol of a strong economy.

Charging Bull, north of Bowling Green
Inset: Brokers, New York Stock Exchange
Detail: Buttonwood Agreement

In the early 1790s, twenty-four brokers met under a buttonwood tree and agreed to trade stocks only with each other. Their pact, the Buttonwood Agreement, founded New York's first official stock exchange.

Coney's Cyclone carries courageous kids.

FEATURING ROLLER COASTERS, gravity-defying rides, side shows, and beaches, Coney Island was the "World's Largest Playground" during its glory days in the early 1900s. The introduction of the five-cent subway ride in 1920 made Coney Island accessible to all. The legendary Cyclone, a wooden roller coaster with sharp turns, steep drops, and speeds up to sixty miles per hour, still offers rides to the brave of heart.

Postcards were popular souvenirs during the early 1900s. On one summer day in 1906, two hundred thousand postcards were sent from Coney Island!

Cyclone, Coney Island
Inset: Coney Island, early 1900s
Detail: Postcards

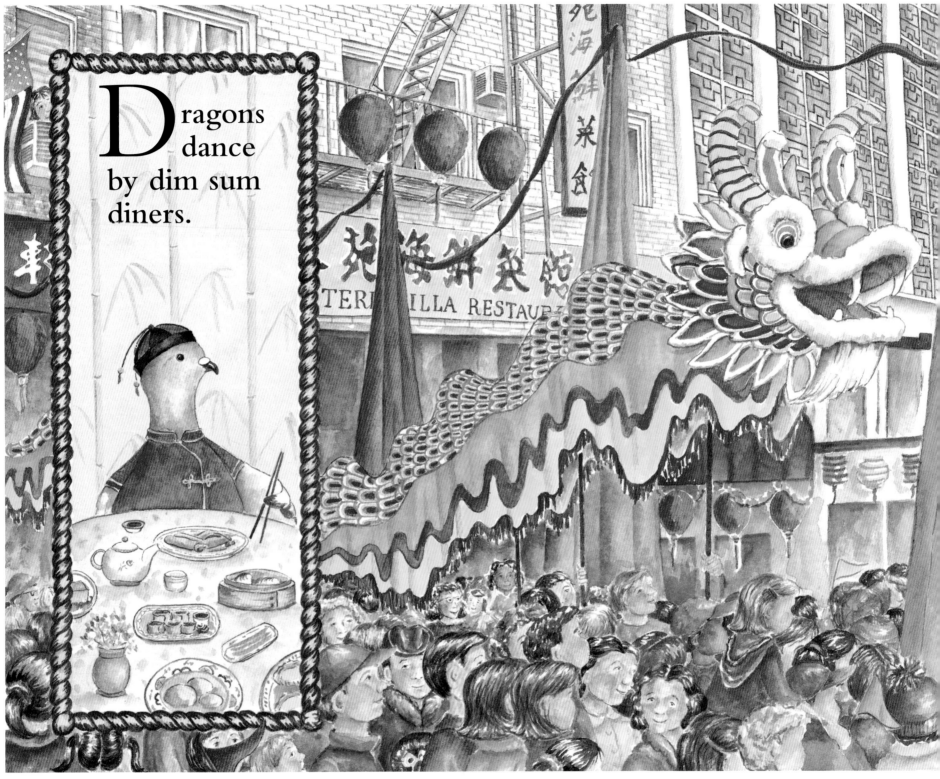

Dragons dance by dim sum diners.

HARSH ANTI-IMMIGRATION LAWS prevented New York's first Chinese immigrants from bringing their families to join them in the United States. When immigration quotas were increased in the 1960s, the community rapidly expanded. Today, Chinatown is a thriving community which maintains many traditional customs. Each winter, the Chinese New Year is celebrated with a festive parade of dancing dragons that symbolize good fortune for the year to come.

Chinese New Year, Chinatown
Inset: Dim Sum
Detail: Chinatown

In Chinatown, phone booths look like pagodas, signs are written in Chinese characters, and ice cream is flavored with lychee and ginger!

Everything is evident from the eighty-sixth floor.

THE INVENTION OF THE ELEVATOR and the use of steel construction allowed New York City to expand in a new direction—upward! Built in just over a year, the Empire State Building was the world's tallest building from 1931 to 1973. At night, its upper stories illuminate the sky with colored lights honoring different holidays. On a clear day, you can see all five boroughs and parts of five states from the observation decks on the 86th and 102nd floors.

Many skyscrapers don't have a 13th floor. No one wants to be on an unlucky floor!

Empire State Building, eighty-sixth floor
Inset: Empire State Building at night
Detail: Elevator buttons

Fifth Avenue is famous for fashion.

During the 1890s, fashionable ladies wore dresses with puffed sleeves and long skirts.

Fashionable gentlemen were not considered properly dressed without jacket, waistcoat (vest), and tie.

"LADIES' MILE," the area around Fifth Avenue from 8th to 23rd Street, was the fashionable shopping district in New York City during the late 1800s. Women in bustling skirts and men with waxed mustaches arrived by horse-drawn carriage to buy the finest luxury goods. As time passed, people moved uptown, and fashionable stores soon followed. Today Fifth Avenue from 40th to 60th Street is one of the busiest shopping areas in the world.

Saks Fifth Avenue
Inset: Fashionable clothes of the 1800s
Detail: Teddy bear

When a Brooklyn manufacturer learned that President Theodore "Teddy" Roosevelt spared a young bear while hunting, he created a plush bear called "Teddy's Bear" in his honor.

Gorgeous gardens grace glass-houses.

Hemlock

Ash

Maple

Oak

THE NEW YORK BOTANICAL GARDEN contains the only surviving section of the maple, hemlock, oak, and ash forest that once covered New York City. The garden is a museum of living plants displayed in gardens, landscapes, and special seasonal exhibits. Within the grounds, a glorious glasshouse glistening with seventeen thousand panes of glass contains plants from around the world that flourish in re-created natural habitats.

Because land is scarce, New Yorkers have to be inventive with their gardens. Plants can be seen sprouting from window boxes, rooftops, and community gardens.

The New York Botanical Garden
Inset: Original forest, New York City
Detail: Everett Children's Adventure Garden, N.Y. Botanical Garden

Heroes are honored on the Hudson.

USS INTREPID, a 42,000-ton, 893-foot-long aircraft carrier, was launched in 1943 and served the US Navy for 31 years. Now a museum docked at Pier 86 on the Hudson River, the vessel offers a glimpse of what life was like for the brave heroes who fought to preserve the peace of our nation. An A-12 Blackbird spy plane, built in 1962, is displayed on the flight deck. It remains one of the fastest planes in the world and is the largest single-seat plane ever built.

USS Intrepid, Hudson River
Inset: Sailor statue
Detail: *Turtle*, USS *Growler*

The Revolutionary War submarine *Turtle* (left) is tiny compared to the USS *Growler* (right), a strategic-missile submarine built in 1958.

Immigrants imagine a better life.

THE STATUE OF LIBERTY is a welcoming symbol of freedom and hope for millions of immigrants arriving in this country. Newcomers from all over the world seek freedom and financial opportunity in the United States. In 1892 Ellis Island opened as an immigration station to accommodate the increasing number of new arrivals. It processed over twelve million people, sometimes up to five thousand a day, until it closed in 1954.

Hopeful new arrivals were examined for disease or disability before they were granted entry into the United States. Although a small percentage failed to pass the medical exam, the fear of being sent back earned the island the nickname "Isle of Tears."

Statue of Liberty
Inset: Immigrants arriving at Ellis Island
Detail: Medical exam, Ellis Island

Journalists jot juicy jargon.

NEW YORK HAS BEEN A CENTER FOR JOURNALISM since the city's first newspaper, the *Gazette*, was printed in 1725. In colonial times, John Peter Zenger, an editor for the *New York Weekly Journal*, was sent to jail for printing criticism of the government. His acquittal on these charges in 1734 helped establish freedom of the press.

When the *New York Times* moved its offices to Times Square in 1904, they celebrated with a rooftop extravaganza on New Year's Eve. The tradition continues each year as an illuminated crystal ball is lowered at the top of One Times Square.

Newsstand, Times Square
Inset: Times Square
Detail: New Year's Eve, Times Square

King Kong, kick lines, and Christmas keep crowds coming.

WHEN RADIO CITY MUSIC HALL opened in 1932, patrons marveled at the nearly six-thousand-seat theater and fancy Art Deco interior. With its huge screen and stage, the theater became a popular location for first-run movies and live shows featuring the Rockettes. Such hit films as *King Kong*, *Mary Poppins*, and *101 Dalmations* have premiered here. Today, the hall is used for concerts, shows, and the ever-exciting Christmas and Easter Spectaculars.

The Rockettes are a precision dance team who are famous for dancing and kicking in a long line.

Radio City Music Hall
Inset: King Kong
Detail: Rockettes

Longshoremen loaded ships in lower Manhattan.

WAVERTREE
19 08
LIVERPOOL

PIER 17
STORE

AFTER THE ERIE CANAL OPENED IN 1825, connecting New York to the heartland, Manhattan became the most important port in the United States. Ships from all over the world arrived at the many docks surrounding the island. In colonial times, ships bringing supplies were greeted with cries for "men 'long shore!" These men, who became known as longshoremen, would leave their regular occupations to load and unload ships.

South Street Seaport
Inset: Crew of the *Wavertree*, 1908
Detail: Fish and seashells

The natural placement of the East River and Hudson River made New York Harbor a plentiful fishing ground.

THE SOUTH STREET SEAPORT MUSEUM, a "museum without walls," preserves New York's seagoing past. The area is still a working port. The buildings of Schermerhorn Row, once counting houses, now house shops, restaurants, and part of the seaport museum's permanent collection. Visitors can glimpse sailors' lives by climbing aboard historic ships and can enjoy a scenic harbor cruise, watch model boat builders and ship carvers ply their trade, and see a working print shop.

Street performers called "buskers"—jugglers, musicians and acrobats—entertain delighted crowds on the piers.

Meteorites, mammals, and minerals meet at the museum.

VISITORS TO THE AMERICAN MUSEUM OF NATURAL HISTORY can go on safari, see a life-size model of a blue whale (the world's largest mammal), stare in awe at a mother Barosaurus protecting her young, and travel to outer space—all in a day! Since it opened in 1869 with a few hundred mounted birds and mammals on display, the museum has gathered the world's largest collection of natural treasures.

American Museum of Natural History
Inset: Barosaurus
Detail: The Star of India

The Star of India, a giant blue sapphire on display at the museum, weighs 563 carats and is worth $450 million.

Notes of *The Nutcracker* dance through the night.

LINCOLN CENTER is the largest performing arts complex in the world. It is home to the Metropolitan Opera, the New York City Ballet, and the New York Philharmonic. In winter, families enjoy *The Nutcracker*, a ballet choreographed by George Balanchine, one of the founders of the New York City Ballet. Balanchine said he wanted people to see the music and hear the dance. In summer, crowds dance beneath the moon at Midsummer Night Swing.

West Side Story, a musical based on Shakespeare's Romeo and Juliet, was set in the neighborhood where Lincoln Center now stands.

Lincoln Center
Inset: *The Nutcracker*
Detail: New York Philharmonic

Olmsted and Vaux created an oblong oasis.

PARKS ARE A WELCOME OASIS FOR NEW YORKERS, most of whom live in apartment buildings that don't have back yards. As New York became more and more crowded in the mid-1800s, the city purchased 843 acres of undeveloped wasteland and started a contest for the best park design. The Greensward Plan, created by Frederick Law Olmsted and Calvert Vaux, was chosen from among thirty-three entries.

Bethesda Fountain, Central Park
Inset: Central Park map
Detail: Fashionable ladies and gents

The Mall, which ends at the Bethesda Fountain, was a place for fashionable ladies and gentlemen to see and be seen during the early 1900s.

DURING THE CONSTRUCTION OF CENTRAL PARK, many people living in shantytowns had to be displaced, swamps were drained, and more than four million trees, shrubs, and plants were brought in. With rowboats, hiking trails, and theater, the park offers fun for everyone. Today, the Central Park Conservancy keeps this public treasure as beautiful and enjoyable as ever.

To discourage buggy racing, a popular sport of the late 1800s, the road in Central Park was deliberately designed with many twists and turns!

Populations in peril are protected and preserved.

Mauritius Pink Pigeon

Red Panda

Snow Leopard

SINCE IT OPENED IN 1899, the Bronx Zoo has been dedicated to protecting animals around the world and is home to over six thousand animals. It was one of the first zoos to exhibit animals in re-creations of their natural habitats when it opened the African Plains exhibit in 1941. Since then, many other habitats have been created, including the Congo Gorilla Forest, Wild Asia, and the World of Darkness.

Bronx Zoo
Inset: Endangered animals
Detail: Gorillas

At the Bronx Zoo, kids can experience how animals live by climbing on a spider web, riding the Bengali Express, trekking through the Congo Gorilla Forest and seeing how bats fly at night.

Quilts of culture quickly covered the city.

IMMIGRANTS TO NEW YORK settled in ethnic neighborhoods, bringing with them customs and traditions from the countries they had left behind. Many settled in four- to six-story tenement buildings on the Lower East Side, which was the most culturally diverse area of New York City. Often arriving with only hope in their pockets, they braved difficult living and working conditions to provide opportunities for their families.

Many immigrants became pushcart vendors, peddling their wares on cobblestone streets. With hard work, some opened stores of their own.

Guss' Pickles, Lower East Side
Inset: Lower East Side Tenement Museum
Detail: Pushcart

R oebling's rope wires reach across the river.

NEW YORK CITY EXPANDED as bridges, subways, ferries, and tunnels gradually linked the four outer boroughs to Manhattan. In 1810, Cornelius Vanderbilt, a sixteen-year-old entrepreneur, established the Staten Island Ferry. When the Brooklyn Bridge opened in 1883, it was the world's longest steel suspension bridge. The design by John Roebling and his son Washington took six hundred workers fourteen years of hazardous labor to complete.

Brooklyn Bridge
Inset: Staten Island Ferry
Detail: Subway

The MTA's (Metropolitan Transportation Authority's) subways, buses, and railroads transport 2.3 billion people a year all over town!

S pectators smile as Snoopy skates by.

EACH NOVEMBER, rain or shine, the Macy's Thanksgiving Day Parade kicks off the holiday season. The parade began in the 1920s, when many Macy's employees were immigrants and proud new Americans. They honored Thanksgiving with a parade of floats, costumes, and bands that recalled the festivals they had enjoyed in their native lands.

In 1927, Felix the Cat was the first balloon to be featured in the parade. Each year the parade includes more and more elaborate balloons of well-loved children's characters.

Macy's Thanksgiving Day Parade
Inset: Channel Gardens, Rockefeller Center
Detail: Parade floats

Tough times take team-work.

WHEN TERRORISTS STRUCK THE WORLD TRADE CENTER on September 11, 2001, New York's brave police force and firefighters sprang into action. Working around the clock, they heroically risked their lives to save others. The Unisphere, a steel sculpture created for the 1964 World's Fair, stands as a symbol of "peace through understanding." The courage of our heroes, and the messages of our monuments remind us of this important goal.

Unisphere, Flushing Meadows-Corona Park
Inset: Twin Towers
Detail: New York City Fire Museum

In 1658, the city's first fire company, the "rattle-watch," was established. Upon spotting a fire, patrolmen would call the alarm by swinging rattles, and run for water buckets. Everyone was expected to come out and help.

U nited
Nations
delegates unite
for universal
understanding.

THE UNITED NATIONS was founded in 1945 to help preserve peace throughout the world. The headquarters on the East River is an international zone with its own stamps and post office. It is not governed by the United States or any other country. Representatives from 189 nations meet every year to discuss the world's most pressing problems. Flags from member countries, arranged in alphabetical order, fly in front of the complex.

UNICEF, an agency of the United Nations, is committed to making the world a better place for children and families.

United Nations Headquarters
Inset: General Assembly
Detail: UNICEF

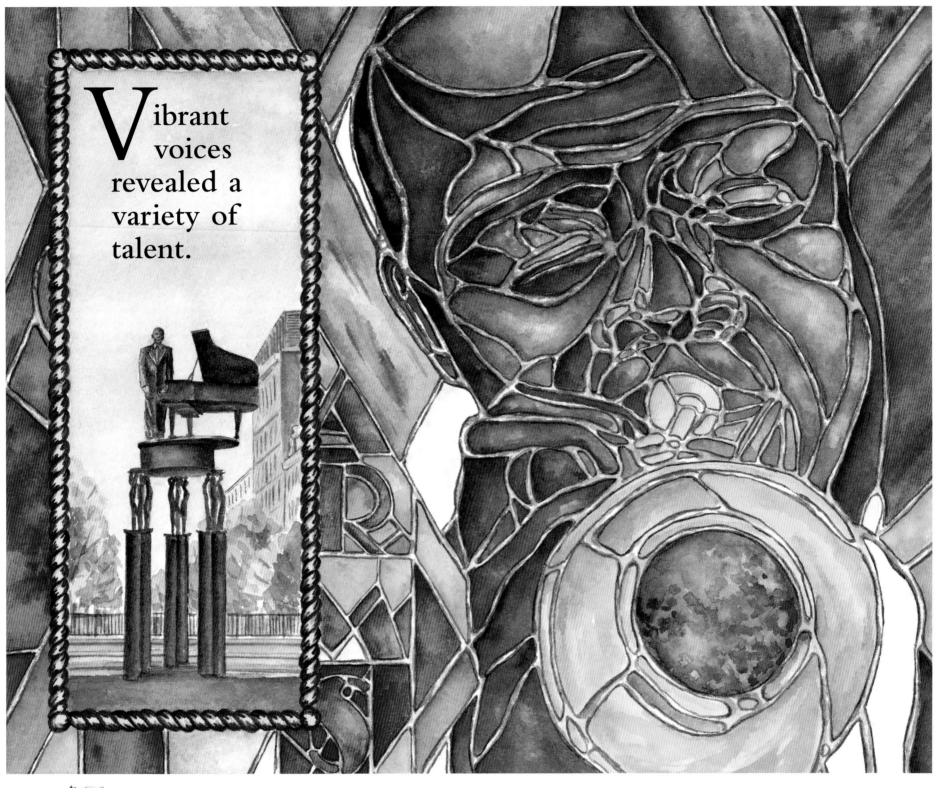

Vibrant voices revealed a variety of talent.

DURING THE 1920S AND 1930S, Harlem saw a burst of creativity known as the "Harlem Renaissance." Through music, poetry, literature, and art, new voices eloquently described the African-American experience. Many theaters and nightclubs that featured black performers did not admit black patrons. Frank Schiffman changed that when he opened the doors of his Apollo Theater to all audiences in the 1930s.

Louis Armstrong stained glass window, The Cotton Club
Inset: Duke Ellington statue
Detail: Apollo Theater

Wednesday night is Amateur Night at the Apollo. Audience enthusiasm has launched the careers of many performers.

Worldwide wonders await in the wings.

FIFTH AVENUE BETWEEN 79TH AND 104TH STREETS was once called "Millionaire's Row" because it was lined with mansions built by New York's most wealthy citizens. The area is now called "Museum Mile," because many museums occupy the former mansions. The Metropolitan Museum of Art is the largest museum, with nearly three million objects collected from all over the world.

The Guggenheim Museum, the Cooper-Hewitt Museum of Design, the Jewish Museum, the International Center of Photography, the Museum of the City of New York, and El Museo del Barrio are among the many fine institutions located on Museum Mile.

Medieval Wing, The Met
Inset: Metropolitan Museum of Art
Detail: Egyptian Galleries, The Met

E**X**otic creatures are exalted each year.

STARTED IN 1892, the still-unfinished Cathedral Church of St. John the Divine is a house of prayer for all people. The cathedral is a living monument with altars, bays, and chapels dedicated to culture, world peace, and the environment. On the Feast of St. Francis each October, animals are brought to the altar and blessed in honor of the saint who loved animals and nature.

The *Seven Generations* statue in the cathedral gardens was inspired by an Iroquois belief that we should consider how our actions will affect the seven generations of children to come.

St. Francis Day, The Cathedral Church of St. John the Divine
Inset: Peace statue
Detail: *Seven Generations* statue

Yankee fans yell yeah!

YANKEE STADIUM, nicknamed "The House that Ruth Built," opened in the Bronx on April 18, 1923, four years after the team bought slugger Babe Ruth from the Boston Red Sox. On opening day, "The Babe" hit a three-run homer as the Yankees coasted to a 4-1 win against his former team. When a New York team wins an important championship, the city celebrates with a tickertape parade through the "canyon of heroes" in lower Manhattan.

Loved for their personalities as well as their skill, the New York Yankees have won more World Series championships than any other team in baseball history.

Yankee Stadium
Inset: Tickertape parade
Detail: Baseball cards

Zillions of commuters zip beneath the zodiac.

BUILT BY CORNELIUS VANDERBILT during the glory days of long-distance train travel, Grand Central Terminal opened in 1913. With support from preservationists like Jacqueline Kennedy Onassis, it has been beautifully restored and listed as a national historic landmark. Grand Central remains a gateway to the city, with half a million commuters each day dashing beneath the vast, vaulted ceiling which is painted with constellations of the zodiac.

Grand Central Terminal
Inset: Subway commuters
Detail: Whispering Gallery

A whisper in the corner of the Whispering Gallery, outside Grand Central's Oyster Bar, can be heard in the opposite corner.

Doorman

Eloise at the Plaza

Flatiron Building

"Imagine"

Jump Rope

Nathan's

One Way

Pretzel

Sculpture

Tiffany & Co.

eXercise

Yellow Cab

Zschock

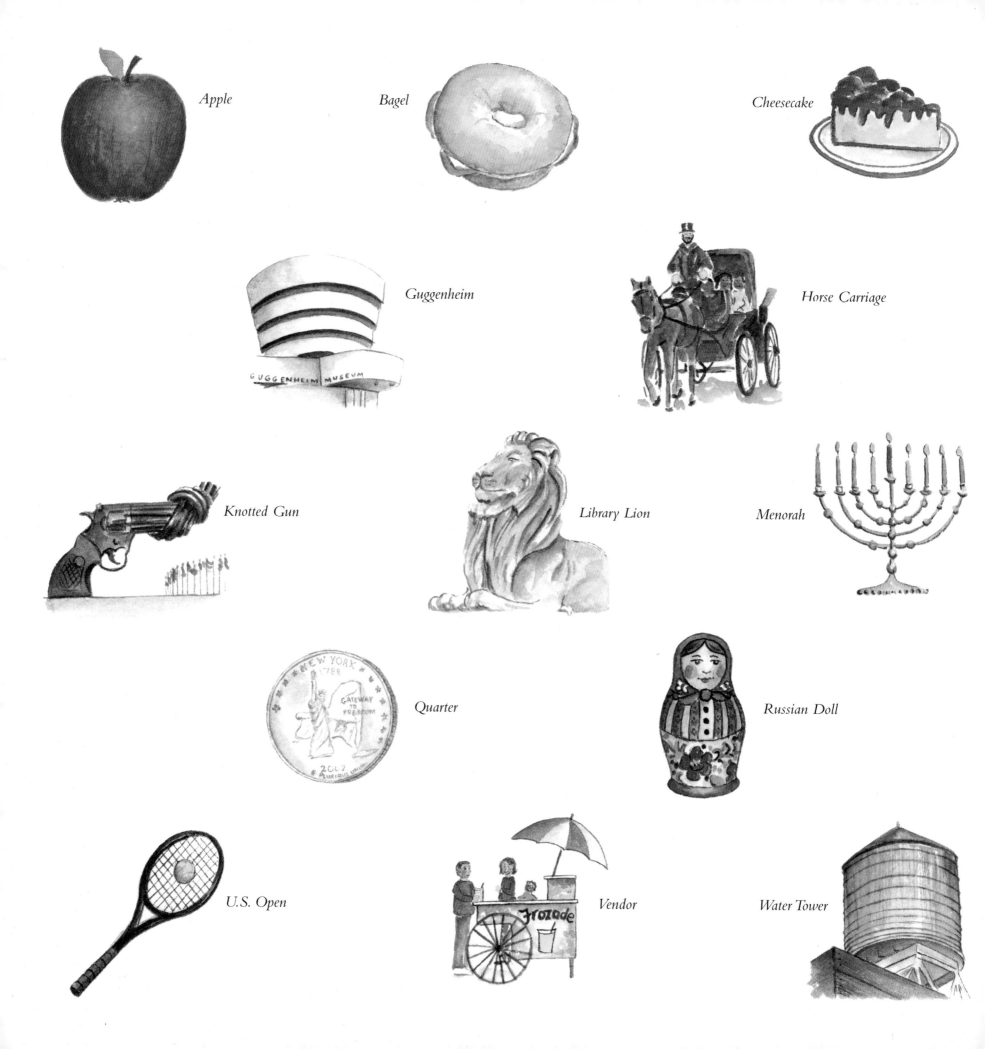

Apple

Bagel

Cheesecake

Guggenheim

Horse Carriage

Knotted Gun

Library Lion

Menorah

Quarter

Russian Doll

U.S. Open

Vendor

Water Tower